Original title:
Snowfall Serenade

Copyright © 2024 Swan Charm
All rights reserved.

Author: Liisi Lendorav
ISBN HARDBACK: 978-9916-79-783-9
ISBN PAPERBACK: 978-9916-79-784-6
ISBN EBOOK: 978-9916-79-785-3

Echoes of the Snow

Whispers through the silent night,
Footsteps hush, a gentle flight.
Blankets soft, a world anew,
Echoes call, the sky so blue.

Snowflakes drift, like dreams unfurl,
Carving paths in winter's swirl.
Every breath, a frosted sigh,
Echoes linger, the stars reply.

Winter's Softest Song

A melody of soft, white grace,
Wraps the land in a warm embrace.
Notes of chill, whispers so sweet,
Winter sings beneath our feet.

Trees adorned with glistening light,
Every branch a pure delight.
In the hush, the song takes flight,
Winter's breath in the soft twilight.

Dances on Ice

Footloose spirits on the lake,
Gliding swiftly as snowflakes break.
Laughter rings beneath the sky,
As stars above twinkle and sigh.

Swirling skirts in the frosty air,
Ballet dreams without a care.
Each turn a graceful, glimmering trace,
Footsteps echo in time and space.

Enchanted Winter Scape

In forests deep, the silence reigns,
Whispers of magic in frosty chains.
Every branch, a tale to tell,
In enchanted winters where dreams dwell.

Icicles shimmer, a delicate lace,
Nature's jewels in a timeless space.
Snow-dusted paths lead away from haze,
To secret realms of wonder and praise.

Glistening fields beneath soft skies,
Where every snowflake brings surprise.
In a winter's embrace, we pause and see,
The beauty of life, wild and free.

Chilling Melodies

Whispers in the twilight,
Soft notes on the breeze.
Moonlight dances lightly,
As the world at ease.

Frozen trees in silence,
Echoes of the night.
Harmony of stillness,
Stars in purest light.

Footprints in the snow,
Stories yet untold.
Each step a soft secret,
In the winter's cold.

Gentle winds they carry,
Songs from years gone by.
Nature sings a chorus,
Beneath the vast sky.

In this serene moment,
Time seems to suspend.
Chilling melodies play,
As the night won't end.

Frosty Night's Embrace

Underneath the blanket,
Of soft, shimmering ice.
The world wrapped in stillness,
A tranquil paradise.

Stars twinkle above,
In the vast cosmic sea.
Glistening like diamonds,
In the chill's decree.

Each breath a white whisper,
In the frosty air.
Nature holds an echo,
Of the night's cool stare.

Shadows dance on snow,
With the moon's silver grin.
In this frosty embrace,
A new tale begins.

Wrapped in nature's warmth,
Cocooned in gentle freeze.
Frosty night's embrace,
Brings profound peace.

Crystal Flakes Descend

Through the still air gliding,
Crystal flakes descend.
Softly they are falling,
Winter's pure dividend.

A dance of white whispers,
From the heavens high.
Each flake a small story,
Written in the sky.

Blanketing the world,
In a shroud of light.
Transforming every scene,
Into pure delight.

Children laugh and play,
In the sparkling glow.
Caught in this wonder,
As the flurries flow.

Crystal flakes in motion,
A ballet from above.
Filling hearts with warmth,
Wrapped in winter's love.

A Choreography of Cold

Winter paints the landscape,
With strokes of icy blue.
Nature spins to silence,
In this chilly view.

Trees wear coats of frost,
Like jewels in the sun.
A choreography, delicate,
As day is done.

The river flows like crystal,
Through the still, deep night.
Reflecting tiny stars,
In their shimmering light.

As shadows stretch and roam,
Whispers fill the air.
Each moment holds a story,
In the frosty glare.

In this dance of winter,
Life finds its calm hold.
With a gentle cadence,
A choreography of cold.

Ethereal Flakes and Evening Hues

Ethereal flakes drift softly down,
Painting the town in white and brown.
Evening hues wrap the world in grace,
Each whispering breeze finds a quiet place.

Stars awaken in the dusky skies,
While winter's breath, a gentle sighs.
The moonlight dances on fields of snow,
As shadows stretch, and tendrils grow.

In this realm of soft, muted light,
Magic stirs in the chill of night.
Footprints fade in the frosty air,
Leaving behind a dreamer's care.

The Quiet Call of Winter Winds

The quiet call of winter winds,
Carries secrets that nature sends.
Trees stand tall in their crystal coats,
While silence swells, and softly floats.

Winds whisper tales of yesteryears,
Murmurs wrapped in frosty tears.
The world sleeps under a tranquil spell,
In the heart of winter, all is well.

Echoes of laughter from days gone by,
Underneath the vast, swirling sky.
Embracing the chill, we find our peace,
As the quiet call begins to cease.

Cascading Dreams in a Frosty Veil

Cascading dreams in a frosty veil,
Float through whispers of winter's tale.
Frosted trees wear a silvery crown,
As night descends and the sun goes down.

Each flake joins the waltz of slow,
A tapestry spun from ice and snow.
Moonlit paths invite us to roam,
In the serene stillness, we find a home.

Dreams cascade like the stars above,
Wrapped in the warmth of winter's love.
Embers flicker, a gentle light,
Guiding us through this tranquil night.

Twilight Serenade of Winter's Heart

Twilight serenade of winter's heart,
Sings to us as the day departs.
Softly it murmurs, tender and bright,
Holding the dusk in a warm embrace tight.

A symphony sung by the chilly breeze,
Rustling leaves from slumbering trees.
In the hush, where shadows play,
Winter's whispers guide our way.

Embracing peace as twilight descends,
With every note, our spirit mends.
Under the stars, we gently sway,
In winter's heart, forever we'll stay.

A Chill in the Breeze of Time

A whisper rides the autumn air,
Leaves dance slowly, full of care.
Moments drift like fragile dreams,
Lost in echoes, or so it seems.

Time meanders, soft and slow,
Carving paths where shadows grow.
Memories linger, bittersweet,
Footsteps fading, yet they greet.

The horizon glows with fading light,
Day embraces the coming night.
In the stillness, hearts align,
Savoring the chill of time.

Whispers weave through silent trees,
Carrying tales upon the breeze.
With every sigh, the moments chime,
In the chill of the breeze of time.

Soft Crystals Beneath the Still Moon

In the night, soft crystals gleam,
Beneath the moon's silver dream.
Snowflakes whisper secrets bright,
Dancing in the calm of night.

Each flake a gem, unique in form,
Weaving frost, a quiet storm.
Nature's art in stillness shines,
Crafting beauty in soft lines.

A tranquil world, wrapped in white,
Embracing magic with delight.
Underneath the watchful moon,
Crystals breathe a gentle tune.

Stillness holds the breath of time,
In this landscape, pure and prime.
Softly, dreams take flight and soar,
Beneath the still moon, evermore.

The Gentle Cadenza of Winter Rain

The winter rain begins to fall,
A tender cadenza, nature's call.
Droplets tap a sweet refrain,
Melodies lost in winter's pain.

Each note a whisper, soft and low,
On windowpanes, they gently flow.
Shadows play with fleeting light,
As day turns slowly into night.

In quiet corners, silence wraps,
While music weaves through winter's gaps.
The world transformed by rhythmic sound,
In this cadenza, peace is found.

So let the rain compose its song,
Reminding us where we belong.
With every drop, a story's spun,
The winter's cadenza has begun.

Silvery Veils of an Icy Tale

Silvery veils drape the world anew,
An icy tale whispered through the blue.
Each crystal glistens like a star,
Guiding dreams that wander far.

In the hush of frost's embrace,
Nature's wonders find their place.
Beneath the sparkle, secrets hide,
Breath of winter, wide and wide.

Frozen whispers call the day,
Painting visions in soft gray.
The air, a canvas, pure and bright,
Crafted gently in winter's light.

Tales unfold with every breath,
Life dances close to icy death.
Yet within this chilling veil,
Lies the beauty of an icy tale.

The Snowman's Lament

Once a figure of delight,
His carrot nose so bright.
Frosty arms spread wide,
Now he stands, a forlorn guide.

Children laugh and play,
But he knows they won't stay.
As the sun starts to creep,
His heart begins to weep.

Tales of joy once spun,
Now he's fading in the sun.
Smiles turn into sighs,
As the winter slowly dies.

Clothes of wool all askew,
He watches skies turn blue.
What will remain of me,
When spring sets me free?

In the warm breeze's thrall,
He wishes to stand tall.
A fleeting, frosty friend,
Longing for the cold to descend.

Cold Kisses from Above

Gentle flakes float down,
Softly kissing the town.
Whispers in the night,
Snowflakes dancing in flight.

Each one unique in grace,
Filling winter's embrace.
A shiver down the spine,
As stars above brightly shine.

They blanket the earth so white,
Turning darkness into light.
With each chilly kiss,
Winter wraps us in bliss.

Silent laughter fills the air,
As children throw with care.
Snowballs fly through the sky,
Underneath the cold, gray high.

Yet in this frozen glow,
A warmth begins to grow.
Soft as dreams that weave,
In the snow, we believe.

Frozen Whispers

In the hush of the night,
Frosted secrets take flight.
Whispers through the trees,
Carried gently by the breeze.

Tales of winter's charm,
Wrapped in a chilling arm.
Moonlight on the snow,
Guiding all below.

Each flake tells a story,
Of love, loss, and glory.
Silent thoughts unwind,
In the cold, softly kind.

As shadows stretch and play,
Dreams drift far away.
In the stillness of frost,
We find what we thought lost.

Echoes of the past,
In every breath we cast.
Underneath the quiet sky,
Frozen whispers softly lie.

Shadows on a Blanket of White

Footsteps fade into night,
Leaving shadows in flight.
A blanket pure and bright,
Covers the world in white.

Moonbeams glisten and gleam,
Casting a silver dream.
Figures drift and sway,
In the stillness, they play.

Branches bow with snow,
In the quiet below.
Each flake a tale untold,
In the night, brave and bold.

The crunch of solitude,
Wrapped in winter's mood.
Hearts beat soft and slow,
Underneath the sprawling glow.

As dawn's light breaks free,
Painting the world to see.
Shadows dance and merge,
On this white winter surge.

Flickering Lights in the Snow

In the quiet night, they glow,
Tiny flames in frozen flow.
Dancing softly, a warm delight,
Guiding souls through the frigid night.

Whispers of joy in the air,
Shimmering dreams without a care.
Each step taken, a gentle sweep,
As the world falls soft, lulled to sleep.

Snowflakes fall like silken threads,
Blanketing paths where no one treads.
Underneath the stars so bright,
Flickering lights steal the night.

Voices carried by winter's breeze,
Warmth remains beneath the freeze.
Together we twinkle, hearts aglow,
In this wonderland draped in snow.

Beneath the moon, our hopes ignite,
As we cherish this stunning sight.
In every flake, a story told,
In flickering lights, our dreams unfold.

The Stillness of December

December drapes her coat of white,
A silent world in soft moonlight.
Not a whisper breaks the peace,
In this moment, time finds ease.

Frosty breath hangs in the air,
Nature pauses, entranced in stare.
The trees wear crystals, pure and bright,
In a hush that feels just right.

Footprints left on untouched snow,
Mark the path where wanderers go.
Each sound muffled, lost in trance,
In stillness, the heart learns to dance.

The chill wraps tightly, comforts near,
In this solitude, we draw near.
As shadows play in the silver glow,
December's love begins to flow.

When the sun dips low, all is still,
A tranquil calm, a thoughtful thrill.
In the darkness, warmth resides,
December's peace, where hope abides.

Whispers of Winter's Embrace

Winter wraps all in her embrace,
A gentle touch, a soothing space.
Softly whispers through the pines,
In her arms, the world aligns.

Each breath a cloud, a frosty plume,
In this quiet, life starts to bloom.
Snowflakes spiral, silent and light,
Whirling dreams in the quiet night.

Bare branches sway in the cold air,
Nature's beauty, raw and rare.
Echoes glide on the chilly breeze,
Carrying secrets among the trees.

Stars peek down with a twinkling smile,
Inviting us to linger a while.
Underneath the velvet sky,
Winter's charm makes the heart sigh.

In her hush, we find our way,
Guided by the light of day.
Embracing moments, sweet and pure,
In winter's hold, our spirits cure.

Chilling Lullabies Beneath the Stars

Under twinkling skies so vast,
Whispers of night call us to rest.
Wrapped in blankets, hearts entwined,
We find solace, peace of mind.

Crackling fires flicker low,
Casting shadows, soft and slow.
With every glance at the night's charm,
We gather close, embraced by warm.

Lullabies sung by the winter's chill,
Calming echoes, a soothing thrill.
As sleepy eyes begin to close,
We drift away, where dreams compose.

Frozen air, crisp as the light,
Guiding dreams into the night.
Beneath the stars, our worries wane,
In chilling whispers, we remain.

As night deepens, still we stay,
In wonderment, we lose our way.
Embraced by winter, hand in hand,
We gather stories, soft as sand.

Droplets of Light on a Winter Evening

Softly the sun descends,
Painting hues of gold and red.
Droplets shimmer like stars,
On branches where they gently spread.

Whispers of the evening breeze,
Echo through the frost-kissed air.
Each drop a fleeting moment,
Of beauty both delicate and rare.

Glistening pearls on frozen ground,
Reflecting dreams in twilight's glow.
A dance of light in shadows found,
Telling tales only night will show.

With every heartbeat of the night,
The world holds its breath in peace.
Under the cloak of fading light,
Winter's magic will never cease.

As night wraps the day in silver,
And the moon begins to rise.
Droplets of light flicker and sliver,
In the canvas of winter skies.

Frosted Fantasies at Dusk

Across the field a soft hush falls,
Frosted whispers greet the trees.
Magic lingers in the air,
Dancing on the chilled night breeze.

Shadows stretch beneath the glow,
Of a fading sun on the hill.
Dreams take flight on frosty wings,
In the quiet, time stands still.

A tapestry of crystal blooms,
Adorns each branch in purest white.
In this realm of silver dreams,
Even darkness feels delight.

Waltzing lights on every surface,
Reflecting hope, a fleeting sigh.
Frosted fantasies entwined with night,
As stars begin to softly cry.

Embraced by winter's gentle hand,
We find solace in this peace.
The world in silence, grand and grand,
As dusk unfolds, all troubles cease.

Quiet Elegance of Silverflakes

Softly falling, silver flakes,
Transforming earth into a dream.
Whispers of elegance in white,
In nature's symphony, we gleam.

Beneath the moon's soft, watchful eye,
Each flake a timeless, fleeting grace.
They twirl and dance, then gently lie,
In quietude, they find their place.

Branches bow with snowy crowns,
A hush envelops all around.
In this serene and tranquil town,
Every heartbeat is the sound.

A canvas fresh with winter's touch,
Each moment wrapped in stillness pure.
Silverflakes whisper calm and hush,
A sacred space, forever sure.

As night reveals its starry cloak,
The world is draped in gentle light.
In quiet elegance, dreams evoke,
A promise held within the night.

Echoing Stillness of Winter's Breath

In the hush of winter's breath,
Silence speaks in softest tones.
Each moment feels like timelessness,
Echoing through nature's bones.

Frosted whispers in the twilight,
Capture shadows in a dance.
Nature's symphony takes flight,
In the glow of a sun-kissed chance.

Crystalline boughs reach to the sky,
Veils of mist weave through the night.
In the stillness, we hear the sigh,
Of dreams awoken in their flight.

Stars emerge, like scattered gems,
Flickering on a velvet sea.
In this tapestry, light condemns,
The chill, inviting warmth to be.

Winter's breath, a gentle song,
Wraps the world in peace profound.
In echoing stillness, we belong,
Here, where love and hope abound.

Whispers of Winter

The snowflakes dance in silence,
A soft, elusive ballet.
Whispers echo through the branches,
As daylight fades away.

Frosty breath upon the window,
Stories woven in the night.
Shadows flicker, memories linger,
Underneath the pale moonlight.

Icicles hang like crystal tears,
Glistening in twilight's grace.
Nature rests in quiet slumber,
Embraced in winter's embrace.

Footsteps crunch on snowy pathways,
A tapestry of white unfurls.
Awakening the quiet beauty,
In a world of icy pearls.

Time slows down in this still moment,
Wrapped in blankets, dreams take flight.
Whispers of winter softly cradle,
The heart beneath the night.

Echoing Stillness of Winter's Breath

In the hush of winter's breath,
Silence speaks in softest tones.
Each moment feels like timelessness,
Echoing through nature's bones.

Frosted whispers in the twilight,
Capture shadows in a dance.
Nature's symphony takes flight,
In the glow of a sun-kissed chance.

Crystalline boughs reach to the sky,
Veils of mist weave through the night.
In the stillness, we hear the sigh,
Of dreams awoken in their flight.

Stars emerge, like scattered gems,
Flickering on a velvet sea.
In this tapestry, light condemns,
The chill, inviting warmth to be.

Winter's breath, a gentle song,
Wraps the world in peace profound.
In echoing stillness, we belong,
Here, where love and hope abound.

Whispers of Winter

The snowflakes dance in silence,
A soft, elusive ballet.
Whispers echo through the branches,
As daylight fades away.

Frosty breath upon the window,
Stories woven in the night.
Shadows flicker, memories linger,
Underneath the pale moonlight.

Icicles hang like crystal tears,
Glistening in twilight's grace.
Nature rests in quiet slumber,
Embraced in winter's embrace.

Footsteps crunch on snowy pathways,
A tapestry of white unfurls.
Awakening the quiet beauty,
In a world of icy pearls.

Time slows down in this still moment,
Wrapped in blankets, dreams take flight.
Whispers of winter softly cradle,
The heart beneath the night.

Frosted Dreams

In the hush of the frosted morning,
Dreams take shape with every breath.
A canvas white, untouched by footsteps,
Awaits the sun's gentle caress.

Through the branches, crystals shimmer,
Nature's jewels, pure and bright.
Every flake a whispered promise,
In the chill of fading light.

The world transforms in icy silence,
Magic woven in the air.
Frosted dreams of winter's wonder,
Hang like wishes everywhere.

Candles flicker with their warmth,
Casting shadows on the wall.
In this realm of soft enchantment,
Heartbeats seem to softly stall.

Underneath the starlit heavens,
Nature draws her tranquil breath.
Frosted dreams weave through the stillness,
Whispering tales of life and death.

Lullabies in White

Gentle snowflakes fall like feathers,
Cloaking all in pristine white.
A lullaby of crisp serenity,
Wraps the world in soft twilight.

Hushed are all the vibrant colors,
Muted by the flurry's grace.
In this dreamscape of the quiet,
Time stands still, a sweet embrace.

Children's laughter fills the morning,
As snowmen rise with joyful cheer.
Lullabies in winter's splendor,
Bringing warmth to hearts so dear.

Each breath released is steam and magic,
Painting patterns in the cold.
Whispers of peace float in the air,
As winter's story unfolds.

In the stillness lies a secret,
Awaiting those who dare to seek.
Lullabies in white will echo,
In the hearts that yearn to speak.

The Silent Blanket

A silent blanket drapes the earth,
Softening edges, blurring lines.
Embracing all in frosted slumber,
Where nature's beauty brightly shines.

Horizon painted in pastel hues,
As dawn breaks with gentle ease.
The world adorned in silver lace,
Wrapped in winter's chilling breeze.

Footsteps muffled by soft cushion,
Whispers of the falling snow.
The hush invites deep reflection,
As moments steadily slow.

Trees stand tall, their branches laden,
With secrets gathered through the night.
In the wonder of the stillness,
Lives a quiet, pure delight.

The silent blanket speaks in volumes,
Of lives intertwined, yet apart.
In its embrace, we find the solace,
That warms the very coldest heart.

Shimmering Silence

In the stillness of the night,
Stars whisper soft delight.
Moonlight dances on the lake,
A tranquil breath, wide awake.

Snowflakes float, a gentle dream,
Crystals glisten, silver beam.
Nature holds her breath so tight,
Wrapped in veils of purest light.

Footsteps echo in the frost,
In the quiet, nothing lost.
Every sound, so crystal clear,
In the silence, I draw near.

Voices hush as shadows creep,
Into this space, I take a leap.
With every pause, the world unwinds,
In shimmering silence, peace I find.

As the night begins to fade,
In this calm, my fears have strayed.
Carry me in soft embrace,
To that still and sacred place.

A Tapestry of White

Blankets stretch across the ground,
Whispers soft without a sound.
Nature dons her purest dress,
In this space, a quiet blessing.

Branches draped in snowy lace,
Every contour finds its grace.
Footprints trace a fleeting path,
In this beauty, feel the math.

Winter's breath, a frosty kiss,
In this chill, there's subtle bliss.
Glistening in morning light,
A tapestry of purest white.

Underneath the icy sheet,
Life awaits, a rhythmic beat.
Time will weave and softly thread,
Spring will rise from winter's bed.

In this moment, still and wide,
Nature's wonders to abide.
A canvas vast, serene, and bright,
Crafted in a tapestry of white.

The Beauty of Hibernation

In the quiet depths of earth,
Life prepares for tranquil birth.
Wrapped in layers, snug and warm,
Finding solace from the storm.

Creatures resting in their dens,
Dream of spring and warmth again.
Fatigue cradled in the dark,
Nature's rhythm leaves its mark.

A pause in time, a gentle fade,
In shadows deep, the world is made.
The beauty found in slowing down,
Beneath the white, the earth's own crown.

Seeds lie dreaming, roots entwined,
In this peace, new life confined.
Hope wrapped tightly, held with care,
Until the sun returns to share.

Beauty blooms in stillness here,
In the waiting, hearts grow clear.
Each breath whispers to the night,
Of hibernation's hidden light.

Whirling Flurries

Twisting winds, a dance begins,
Snowflakes swirl, as laughter spins.
In the hush of winter's breath,
Joy emerges, teasing death.

Spirits rise with every gust,
In the flakes, we place our trust.
Ballets played in frozen air,
Nature paints without a care.

Children giggle, arms outstretched,
Snowball fights, all worries fetched.
Whirling flurries fill the sky,
In their midst, we laugh and fly.

Every flake a tiny song,
Together, where we all belong.
Eyes wide open, hearts aglow,
In the magic, gently flow.

As daylight fades, the dance persists,
Cozy nights wrapped in mist.
Twilight whispers tales of cheer,
In whirling flurries, winter near.

The Winter's Caress in Soft Beats

The frost bites soft on bare skin,
Whispers of chill in the evening glow.
Snowflakes dance as shadows spin,
Nature's lullabies, a gentle flow.

Beneath the stars, a silent prayer,
Each flake a wish that drifts from sea.
Wrapped in blankets, free of care,
Winter's caress, a sweet decree.

The world is hushed, time slowly sways,
Gold and silver hidden by white.
In this stillness, the heart relays,
Soft beats echoing through the night.

Candles flicker, casting dreams,
Stories told in warmth and light.
Winter's caress, soft as it seems,
Embraces hearts till morning bright.

With every gust, a tale unfolds,
Frozen secrets we long to hear.
In winter's grasp, our hopes retold,
A symphony that draws us near.

A Tapestry of Ice and Sound

In the morning light, the world gleams,
A tapestry woven, pure and bright.
Each frost-laden branch and flecked beam,
Crafts a scene of shimmering white.

Beneath the surface, the silence sings,
Crystals glisten, nature's art.
Embroidered whispers as winter clings,
A soft cloak that wraps the heart.

Footfalls crunch on paths of snow,
Each step a note in winter's song.
Echoes mingle, soft and slow,
Creating harmony all along.

Icicles dangle like diamonds fair,
Catch the sun in a playful way.
A canvas draped in frozen air,
Where fleeting beauty holds its sway.

With every breath, our joy expands,
Carved in ice, these moments dear.
In winter's grip, life softly stands,
A tapestry of love and fear.

Sweet Flakes Falling on Listening Ears

Sweet flakes falling, nature's grace,
Softly landing, quiet and fleet.
Whispers flutter, as dreams embrace,
Each gentle touch, a soft heartbeat.

The world transforms, a silver lace,
A blanket warm, inviting peace.
In this magic, we find our place,
As soft wonders begin to cease.

Branches bow with a heavy load,
Nature's weight feels light and free.
In each flake, a story flowed,
Gentle murmurs of memory.

As twilight creeps, the colors fade,
Stars peek through the velvet night.
In winter's arms, we seek the shade,
Of falling flakes, a pure delight.

The world holds its breath, time stands still,
In snowy silence, our hearts align.
Sweet flakes falling, a sacred thrill,
Echoes linger, yours and mine.

Murmurs of Winter's Heartbeat

Murmurs of winter wrap the night,
A breath released into the chill.
Frost-kissed air, a pure delight,
Whispered secrets, soft and still.

The moon hangs low, a watchful eye,
Casting shadows on frozen ground.
Beneath the blanket, soft and shy,
Winter's heartbeat is all around.

Every gust brings tales from afar,
Stories carried on the breeze.
Night unfolds beneath each star,
In its embrace, we find our ease.

The crackle of branches, the silence hums,
Nature's orchestra, pure and clear.
In every heartbeat, winter comes,
With murmurs that draw us near.

As dawn breaks soft, the world awakes,
The echoes linger, memories shared.
In winter's heart, a warmth remakes,
Bound together, lives bared.

Celestial Snowdance

In the night, stars gently fall,
Whispers twirl, they dance for all.
Blankets of white, the earth adorned,
In this stillness, hearts are warmed.

Moonlight glistens on frosted trees,
A hush surrounds, carried by the breeze.
Each flake a secret, a story told,
In the quiet, magic unfolds.

Winter's breath, a chilling sigh,
Under the vast, expanse of sky.
In the silence, time drifts slow,
Caught in the grip of falling snow.

Frozen whispers fill the air,
Peace found in the cold night fair.
Each step taken, soft and light,
Guided gently by silvered light.

Nature smiles, in purest white,
Celestial wonders, pure delight.
In every flake, a world is spun,
As the dance beneath the stars is done.

Murmurs of Winter's Heartbeat

Murmurs of winter wrap the night,
A breath released into the chill.
Frost-kissed air, a pure delight,
Whispered secrets, soft and still.

The moon hangs low, a watchful eye,
Casting shadows on frozen ground.
Beneath the blanket, soft and shy,
Winter's heartbeat is all around.

Every gust brings tales from afar,
Stories carried on the breeze.
Night unfolds beneath each star,
In its embrace, we find our ease.

The crackle of branches, the silence hums,
Nature's orchestra, pure and clear.
In every heartbeat, winter comes,
With murmurs that draw us near.

As dawn breaks soft, the world awakes,
The echoes linger, memories shared.
In winter's heart, a warmth remakes,
Bound together, lives bared.

Celestial Snowdance

In the night, stars gently fall,
Whispers twirl, they dance for all.
Blankets of white, the earth adorned,
In this stillness, hearts are warmed.

Moonlight glistens on frosted trees,
A hush surrounds, carried by the breeze.
Each flake a secret, a story told,
In the quiet, magic unfolds.

Winter's breath, a chilling sigh,
Under the vast, expanse of sky.
In the silence, time drifts slow,
Caught in the grip of falling snow.

Frozen whispers fill the air,
Peace found in the cold night fair.
Each step taken, soft and light,
Guided gently by silvered light.

Nature smiles, in purest white,
Celestial wonders, pure delight.
In every flake, a world is spun,
As the dance beneath the stars is done.

Glimmers of Solitude

In the quiet corner of my mind,
A flicker of peace, a moment to find.
Soft shadows fall, the sun dips low,
In this stillness, feelings flow.

Gentle whispers, secrets untold,
In the embrace, the night turns cold.
Stars begin to twinkle bright,
Guiding thoughts through the endless night.

Reflecting on dreams, lost in the dark,
Finding comfort, a tiny spark.
Solitude wraps like a warm old friend,
In silence, the journey begins to blend.

Time slows down, yet speeds away,
As glimmers of hope in shadows play.
Each heartbeat echoes, soft and low,
In the heart, a quiet glow.

With every breath, I feel alive,
In solitude's realm, I learn to thrive.
Finding joy in moments few,
In the dark, a light breaks through.

The Quietest Season

Whispers of wind in autumn's crest,
Leaves cascade, the trees find rest.
Nature sighs, a gentle close,
In this calm, the spirit grows.

Fading light, the day retreats,
Crispness lingers, as twilight meets.
Soft shadows waltz upon the ground,
In stillness, beauty can be found.

The world wraps in a muted coat,
Echoes of laughter seem to float.
With every step, the earth is hushed,
In this season, time is brushed.

A tapestry woven with colors bright,
The quietest season, a breath of light.
Moments stretch, as days grow short,
In solitude, the heart finds comfort.

Fires crackle, stories shared,
In the warmth, we feel prepared.
Embracing rest, as dreams take flight,
In the glow of this gentle night.

Silent Footsteps

In moonlit hours, where shadows creep,
Silent footsteps tread, the world asleep.
A journey begun under stars aglow,
Each quiet step, where no winds blow.

Through the mist, the path unfolds,
Whispers of dreams that the night holds.
With every heartbeat, adventures await,
In this stillness, we contemplate.

Past the trees, where echoes remain,
Footsteps linger, an unseen claim.
The woods invite, with secrets deep,
In the silence, memories keep.

A gentle breeze carries the past,
Time held still, yet moving fast.
In the night, every shadow speaks,
Silent footsteps, where the heart seeks.

Nature listens to the unvoiced dreams,
In the darkness, the starlight beams.
Here, we wander, drift, and roam,
In silent footsteps, we find our home.

Songs of Solitude Beneath Frosted Skies

In the hush of dawn's embrace,
Whispers curl like smoke in air.
Silence sings in icy lace,
A symphony beyond compare.

Beneath the frost, a world so still,
Echoes dance in shadows long.
Nature pauses, calm and chill,
In solitude, I find my song.

Stars retreat, their watch now done,
As daylight spills in gentle streams.
The quiet hush, a weightless run,
Awakens all my dreams and schemes.

Frozen trees like sentinels stand,
Guarding secrets of the night.
In their branches, grace is planned,
Each twinkle holds the heart's delight.

As I wander, thoughts entwined,
In the crispness, I feel alive.
Among the frost, my soul aligned,
In this solitude, I thrive.

The Enchantment of Chilly Evenings

Dusk descends, a cooling breath,
The air is thick with magic's thread.
Embers glow, resisting death,
While shadows dance, the day has fled.

Frosted fields stretch wide and vast,
Underneath the twilight's spell.
Moments linger, slow and fast,
Each heartbeat tells a story well.

Whispers of the night arise,
Like secrets held in velvet hands.
Moonlight bathes the world in sighs,
Casting dreams upon the plains.

Stars awaken, twinkling bright,
A tapestry of hope and fear.
Chilly evenings stir the night,
Where every breath brings art so clear.

With each breeze, the magic swells,
Enchantment wraps me, soft and tight.
In chilly evenings, heart repels,
The warmth of dreams ignites the night.

Frost-Laden Whispers at Daybreak

Morning breaks, a whispered chill,
Frosty petals kiss the ground.
Nature's breath, it lingers still,
In this hush, a peace profound.

Birds begin their sweet refrain,
Notes that flutter through the gray.
With each sound, a gentle gain,
Frost-laden whispers greet the day.

Sunrise paints the world anew,
Golden hues melt silver frost.
A canvas bright where dreams come true,
In quiet moments, nothing's lost.

As the world stirs from its sleep,
I bask in warmth, the chill abates.
With every secret nature keeps,
A day unfolds, renewed by fates.

In these hours of fleeting grace,
I find my heart and soul align.
Amongst the whispers, time and space,
Frost-laden moments intertwine.

Tranquil Glimmers on a Shimmering Night

Beneath the quilt of midnight's veil,
Soft glimmers dance in endless flight.
Each twinkle tells a timeless tale,
In tranquil wonder, hearts take light.

The moon casts shadows, rich and deep,
Among the trees, a secret glow.
In this calm, the world does sleep,
While stars above begin to flow.

Cool breezes whisper through the leaves,
A lullaby for souls alone.
In this stillness, the heart believes,
In shimmering nights, we're never known.

Each moment holds a fleeting bliss,
As dreams unfurl like evening mist.
In tranquil glimmers, hearts find kiss,
Where love and beauty coalesce.

As dawn approaches, night recedes,
Yet memories linger, soft and light.
In tranquil glimmers, the soul feeds,
On dreams that shine through every night.

The Dance of Frosted Feathers

In the quiet woods they sway,
Frosted feathers drift away,
Caught in whispers of the breeze,
Dancing softly through the trees.

Each flake spins a tale of light,
Beneath the stars, so pure, so bright,
They twirl in harmony and grace,
A fleeting dream in winter's embrace.

As shadows stretch and darkness falls,
The nightingale tenderly calls,
In the moonlight's gentle sway,
Frosted feathers dance and play.

Underneath a cover of white,
Life stirs softly, pure delight,
Frosted wings in soft parade,
Whirling slowly, unafraid.

With every step, the world is new,
Bathed in silver, loved by few,
These magical moments, forevermore,
As frost adorns the winter floor.

Echoes of Ice in Twilight's Glow

Twilight whispers secrets low,
As ice begins its gentle show,
Crystals shimmer, catch the light,
Enchanting all, a wondrous sight.

The air is crisp, filled with dreams,
Each reflection softly beams,
In this twilight's cool embrace,
Echoes linger, time and space.

Frozen branches creak and sigh,
Underneath the pale sky,
Nature's song, a symphony,
In the hush, it sets us free.

Where shadows dance on icy streams,
And the world is full of dreams,
Echoes of the past arise,
Glistening under twilight skies.

With every breath, a story shared,
In the stillness, hearts laid bare,
Echoes of ice in twilight glow,
Hold the magic we all know.

Glistening Silence Wrapped in White

A blanket soft, pure and bright,
Glistening silence, wrapped in white,
Each step an echo, crisp and clear,
In this stillness, winter is near.

The world transformed, a dreamlike scene,
Where everything glistens, fresh and clean,
A symphony played in shadows cast,
Nature's beauty, unsurpassed.

Heartbeats sync with the falling snow,
In quiet moments, spirits grow,
Wonders hidden in each flake,
A peaceful stillness, time to take.

Whispers of the night draw near,
Painting landscapes, crystal clear,
In this embrace, let worries cease,
Wrapped in white, we find our peace.

With every breath, the cold ignites,
A dance of dreams, pure and bright,
Glistening silence, as we unite,
Wrapped in the warmth of winter's light.

A Symphony of Frozen Wonders

In the heart of winter's day,
Frozen wonders come to play,
A symphony of ice and snow,
Marking paths where dreams can flow.

Each crystal sings a unique tune,
Underneath the glowing moon,
Nature's orchestra comes alive,
In this realm, we thrive and strive.

Softly, softly, the breezes hum,
To the rhythm of the drums,
Each flake a note, every gust a sound,
In this beauty, we are found.

As shadows fade and mornings call,
Frozen wonders whisper small,
In a world that sparkles bright,
A symphony throughout the night.

With every heartbeat, let us soar,
Through the magic, we explore,
A symphony of frozen dreams,
Eternal life in frozen streams.

The Delicate Waltz of Snow and Night

Under velvet skies, the snowflakes dance,
Twinkling softly, they take their chance.
With every spin, a silent embrace,
Whispers of magic in the night's grace.

Moonbeams twirl, casting shadows wide,
While frosty breath swirls like a tide.
Each flake a story, pure and bright,
A waltz of wonder painted in white.

Echoes of laughter in the winter air,
Footprints trailing, a secret to share.
Velvet blankets hush the world below,
In this delicate waltz, all hearts aglow.

Stars peek through, glimmering high,
As the night holds its breath, time slips by.
In this serene moment, dreams ignite,
The delicate waltz of snow and night.

A final spin, as dawn starts to break,
The world awakens, gentle and awake.
Yet in our hearts, we keep the glow,
Of the delicate waltz, forever in snow.

Icy Roses Blooming in Silence

In gardens where whispers of frost take root,
Icy roses bloom, a cold tribute.
Petals shimmer like diamonds in light,
Held in the silence of winter's night.

Each breath of wind carries stories untold,
Of love and dreams wrapped in the cold.
With colors fading, their beauty remains,
In crystalline forms, life's gentle chains.

Beneath a blanket of white, they thrive,
In a world where the softest hearts survive.
Yet behind their beauty, a secret does dwell,
Of strength hidden deep, where silence can tell.

As the frost kisses each fragile line,
These icy roses bloom, a sign divine.
In their stillness, the heart finds its way,
Through the chill of winter, in muted display.

Time weaves a tapestry, subtle and sly,
Icy roses blossom, beneath the gray sky.
In their silent elegance, we find our peace,
A moment of beauty, where all worries cease.

Luminous Frostpainting at Dawn

At dawn's first light, the world transforms,
A canvas of frost, nature adorns.
Brush strokes of silver, a whisper so clear,
Luminous beauty, drawing us near.

The sun's warm fingers caress the cold air,
Painting the landscapes with delicate care.
As shadows retreat, the colors arise,
In a frozen embrace where enchantment lies.

Every blade of grass, a glistening gem,
Illuminated softly by nature's own hymn.
With every breath, a new story's spun,
Of dawn's radiant art, a battle won.

Frosted trees stand like guardians tall,
Their branches like lace, a mystical call.
In this moment's grace, we find our song,
In the luminous frostpainting, where we belong.

The day awakens with a gentle sigh,
A promise of warmth as the sun climbs high.
Yet the remnants of night, in beauty, remain,
In the frostpainting at dawn, we find our refrain.

Whispers of Crystal Dreams

In the quiet hours when stars softly gleam,
Whispers arise from the land of dreams.
A tapestry woven with silver and light,
Guiding us gently through the deep night.

Each snowflake falling, a secret unfurled,
A mystical journey to another world.
Where wishes take flight on wings made of gold,
In this crystal realm, our stories unfold.

Beneath the moon's gaze, illusions take form,
A dance of enchantment within the storm.
As echoes of laughter seep into the air,
Whispers of dreams, a magical affair.

Time stands still in this wondrous embrace,
Where every heartbeat finds its own space.
In the hush of the night, we drift and we roam,
In whispers of crystal, we find our way home.

So close your eyes, let your spirit take flight,
To realms of wonder, lost in the night.
In the whispers of dreams, we'll forever stay,
Guided by stars, we'll find our way.

Palettes of Pale

In the dawn where shadows fade,
Whispers of winter start to invade.
Soft hues blend in the silent light,
A canvas born from the still of night.

Gentle blues and grays entwine,
A dance of color, a breath divine.
Frosted branches stretch and sway,
Nature's art in a cool display.

Clouds weave secrets in the sky,
With every stroke, the world complies.
The palette grows with each soft sigh,
Embracing moments that pass us by.

In silence deep, the colors speak,
Fleeting glimpses, both bold and meek.
A tapestry of dreams unfurled,
In winter's grasp, a magic world.

With every snowflake, a story told,
In shades of white and hints of gold.
The artist's heart, a vibrant eye,
Creating beauty as time drifts by.

Frost-kissed Memories

Frosted windows tell a tale,
Of laughter soft, of joy unveiled.
Echoes of warmth in the cold night air,
Whispers of moments we used to share.

With every flake that gently lands,
A memory sparks in frozen strands.
Footprints linger on paths of snow,
Tracing the tales of long ago.

The fire crackles, a warm embrace,
Reflecting glimmers of a familiar face.
As shadows dance, the stories grow,
In the hearth's glow, our spirits flow.

Time stands still in this winter sight,
Wrapped in the hush of the starry night.
Seasons change, but we hold tight,
To frost-kissed memories, pure delight.

Through every winter that comes and goes,
The heart remembers what the cold bestows.
In the depths of chill, we find the spark,
That keeps our memories bright in the dark.

Tales of Winter Air

A breath of chill, a tale begins,
In winter's grasp, the laughter spins.
Stories hang in the crisp, cold breeze,
Carried softly through the frozen trees.

Whispers weave in the twilight glow,
As snowflakes twirl in a silent show.
Each gust of wind a voice of the past,
Echoing moments, meant to last.

The moonlight glimmers on icy streams,
Illuminating all our dreams.
In the stillness, memories spark,
Tales of winter fill the dark.

Children's laughter, a joyous sound,
Skates on ice as their joy resounds.
Frosty breath floats in the night,
As their spirits dance in pure delight.

Through each snowy day and starry sky,
Stories unfold as the seasons fly.
In the heart of winter, tales we share,
In every breath of the winter air.

Luminous Snowflakes

Luminous snowflakes drift and glide,
Delicate dancers with nowhere to hide.
Each one unique, a spark of grace,
Whirling gently in a soft embrace.

Under street lamps, they shimmer bright,
A blanket of white in the still of night.
They glisten softly, a magical sight,
Filling the world with pure delight.

The hush of winter, a tranquil scene,
Frosted gardens, a silvery sheen.
Beneath the moon, they twinkle and play,
Capturing dreams in their gentle display.

Each flake tells a tale, a fleeting wish,
In their descent, the world might miss.
Yet in their landing, calm descends,
A moment of peace, where chaos ends.

When morning comes, they fade away,
But their beauty lingers, a soft ballet.
In the heart's memory, they stay aglow,
These luminous snowflakes, a cherished show.

The Winter's Waltz

Snowflakes twirl in the pale moonlight,
Dancing softly, a shimmering sight.
Whispers of frost in the brisk night air,
Nature's beauty, beyond compare.

Trees stand tall, cloaked in white,
Branches sway, a graceful flight.
Echoes of laughter, children play,
In this winter wonderland, they stay.

Hushed whispers travel with the breeze,
Crimson cheeks as they laugh with ease.
Footprints mark the path they take,
In every step, the joy they make.

A world adorned with glitter and glow,
Every flake tells a story we know.
As the stars twinkle, nights feel long,
Together we sway, a winter song.

As morning breaks, the sun will rise,
Turning landscapes into a surprise.
The dance of winter, a fleeting trance,
Nature's love, in this frosty expanse.

Snowy Reverie

In the hush of the falling snow,
Dreams are whispered, emotions flow.
Blankets of white on rooftops lie,
Softly covering the world, oh my.

Footsteps crunch on a winding lane,
Each step echoes, a gentle refrain.
Children's laughter fills the air,
Joy unbound, without a care.

Snowflakes shimmer, catch the light,
Creating magic with every flight.
Memories loom, cherished and bright,
In the embrace of this serene night.

Fires crackle in homes nearby,
Warmth that sweeps the heart, oh sigh.
A cup of cocoa, shared delight,
In snowy reverie, souls ignite.

As twilight descends, the world will pause,
In stillness, we gather, without cause.
Together we weave dreams anew,
In the snowy night, just me and you.

Icicle Serenade

Icicles hang, a crystal parade,
Reflecting light, an artful cascade.
Winter's breath, chilling and sweet,
Nature orchestrates a delicate beat.

Rustling leaves now hush in sleep,
Beneath the weight of the snow so deep.
Silent whispers from the woods arise,
A serenade sung under starlit skies.

Frosted windows tell tales of old,
Of warmth and love, and hearts of gold.
Each drop from the icicles forms a chime,
A melody that dances through time.

Beneath the glow of a silver moon,
Winter's hush lingers, a gentle tune.
As shadows stretch, we sit and dream,
In this serene, wintry theme.

With each dawn, the icicles gleam,
An ever-changing, enchanting theme.
Nature's song, a timeless embrace,
In icicle serenade, we find our place.

Hushed Tones of the Chill

Hushed tones echo in the crisp night air,
Whispers of winter, a moment rare.
The world sleeps softly, blanketed bright,
Cradled in dreams under shimmering white.

Branches bow low under frosty weight,
A stillness that dances, longing to sate.
The moon casts shadows on the silver ground,
As magic of winter weaves all around.

Each breath, a cloud that softly swirls,
In this quiet, the heart unfurls.
Gentle sighs escape from the trees,
The sound of winter, a tender breeze.

Footsteps linger on the snowy path,
In the chill, each soul finds its math.
A warmth within, despite the freeze,
Binding us close, like the whispered leaves.

As dawn arrives, paints the world anew,
Hushed tones fading, but still we pursue.
Memories linger in the morning glow,
In the chill of winter, love's embers grow.

Quivering Leaves and Crystal Air

In the gentle breeze, leaves sway,
Whispering secrets, they dance and play.
Underneath the fading light,
Nature's canvas, pure delight.

Raindrops linger, kissed by night,
Sparkling like stars, a joyful sight.
Each rustle tells a timeless tale,
Of ancient woods where spirits hail.

Colors fade, yet life remains,
Echoes of the softest rains.
Quivering leaves, a tender song,
In crystal air where dreams belong.

Morning's light, a silken thread,
Weaving whispers where joy is spread.
Underneath the sky so wide,
Nature's art, forever abide.

As twilight wraps the world in peace,
All worries wane, all troubles cease.
In the hush, we find our place,
Among the leaves, in nature's grace.

Celestial Frost on a Quiet Canvas

A blanket soft, the world adorned,
Each surface shines, softly warmed.
Celestial frost, a mystic sight,
Whispers secrets of the night.

The morning sun begins to rise,
Painting gold across the skies.
Every breath, a steamy plume,
Filling hearts with joyful bloom.

Crystals sparkling, nature's art,
Beauty captured, plays its part.
On a canvas, pure and white,
Magic glistens, pure delight.

Winter's breath, an artist's touch,
Frosty patterns, loved so much.
Quiet moments, soft and rare,
In the stillness, beauty's flare.

As day unfolds, the frost will fade,
Yet memories of beauty stayed.
In each heart, a piece remains,
Celestial dreams in soft refrains.

The Melodic Breath of Ice

In the stillness, ice will sing,
Melodies that winter brings.
Frozen rivers, serene and bold,
Whispers of a tale retold.

The crispness dances on the breeze,
Enchanting hearts with gentle ease.
In every shiver, a sweet embrace,
Nature's rhythm, a calming grace.

Underneath the moonlit sky,
Stars above, like dreams that fly.
Crystal branches catch the light,
Glittering softly, pure and bright.

The coldest nights, the warmest glow,
A tranquil peace begins to flow.
In icy breaths, our worries cease,
Harmony found, a deepened peace.

As dawn awakens, shadows fade,
Yet music lingers, softly played.
In every corner of the night,
The melodic breath brings pure delight.

Verses Written in the Frost

A canvas cold, the world in white,
Verses penned in mornings bright.
Frosty whispers, soft caress,
Nature's quill, a pure finesse.

Every window, story told,
Captured moments, bright and bold.
In delicate script, the frost will gleam,
Reflecting life, a waking dream.

As daylight breaks, the magic fades,
Yet traces linger, joy pervades.
Nature writes with gentle hand,
A masterpiece across the land.

Within the chill, a warmth remains,
In every line, the heart attains.
Verses waiting for eyes to see,
The beauty of frost, wild and free.

As time moves on, seasons change,
Memories linger, sweet and strange.
In every breath, the stories flow,
Written in frost, where love will grow.

Luminous Chill in a Midnight Reverie

In shadows deep, the stars align,
Whispers of night, so calm, divine.
A silver glow, a soft embrace,
The chilling breath of time and space.

Beneath the moon, the world lies still,
A tranquil hush, a silent thrill.
Frosted dreams in shimmering blue,
A midnight sky, a canvas new.

The air is sharp, with breath like mist,
Each fleeting moment, not to miss.
Time slows down, as dreams take flight,
In this serene, enchanted night.

Echoes dance where shadows play,
In every sigh, the night turns gray.
With each heartbeat, a story spins,
In luminous chill, the magic begins.

So close your eyes, and breathe it in,
Let the night's sweet whispers begin.
For in this pause, we find our way,
Luminous chill of a timeless stay.

Harmonious Hush of Frosty Twilight

As daylight wanes, a hush descends,
The icy breeze, where silence blends.
Twilight's breath, a gentle sigh,
A symphony beneath the sky.

Glittering flakes in light's last dance,
Nature's art, a pure romance.
Trees stand tall, their crowns adorned,
In frosty beauty, the evening mourned.

The distant call of nightbirds sings,
In this embrace, the heart takes wings.
Every shadow plays its part,
Painting calm in winter's heart.

A tapestry of blue and gray,
Dreams awaken, drift away.
In this harmonic, tranquil sphere,
Frosty twilight holds us near.

So gather close, let warmth ignite,
In winter's calm, we find our light.
For in the hush, our souls will thrive,
Embracing what makes us alive.

Delicate Whispers of the Winter Muse

In frost-kissed air, a secret stirs,
Whispers float like falling furs.
Delicate tales on silence spun,
A winter muse in shadows run.

The world transforms in muted grace,
Each flake unique, a soft embrace.
Beneath the cover of moonlit sheen,
Winter weaves a stunning scene.

As echoes hush, a story forms,
In chilly winds, in peaceful norms.
A melody drifts through slumbering trees,
Carried forth on a gentle breeze.

Worn pathways glow under starlit skies,
Nowhere to rush, just dream and rise.
Through snowy nights, our hearts will muse,
In delicate whispers, we shall choose.

So listen close to winter's breath,
In every moment, find life's depth.
For in these whispers, soft and true,
The winter muse awaits for you.

Frost's Artistry on a Canvas of Night

With every breath, the canvas glows,
Frost's artistry, as each line flows.
Night adorns, with stars in sight,
A breathless dance in the pale moonlight.

Patterns etched on window panes,
Nature's touch in soft refrains.
Every twinkle, a spell is cast,
In the depth of night, our dreams are vast.

Gentle shadows paint the ground,
In hushed tones, a peace unbound.
The world wrapped tight in silver thread,
Where warmth meets cool, where hopes are fed.

Frosty fingers trace the sky,
On whispered winds, we learn to fly.
With each stroke, a magic found,
Artistry that knows no bounds.

So let us wander through this night,
Beneath the stars, we find our light.
In frost's embrace, our souls take flight,
On a canvas bright, in pure delight.

Enigmatic Silence in Chilling Air

In the shadow of twilight's embrace,
Whispers dance in the frosty space.
The stars blink softly in the dark,
Moonlit secrets leave their mark.

Echoes linger, a haunting glow,
Silence swathes the land below.
Each breath forms a crystal sigh,
Painting dreams as night drifts by.

Frosted whispers in the trees,
Carried gently by the breeze.
A stillness wraps the world in peace,
In chilling air, all worries cease.

Mysteries held in the night sky,
Questions linger, almost nigh.
Yet in this silence, I stand still,
Embraced by night's ethereal thrill.

To the dawn, this moment bends,
As silence deepens, night transcends.
With secrets shared in the cold air,
Enigmatic stillness everywhere.

Softer than Winter

Whispers of snow in the pale light,
Drifting softly, taking flight.
A gentle touch on a slumbering earth,
Bringing calm and a quiet rebirth.

Snowflakes kiss the ground with grace,
Stealing warmth from every space.
Like a lullaby, they weave and sway,
A tender song that bids the day.

In frosty air, breath turns to mist,
A silent promise in love's soft tryst.
Underneath the moon's gentle glow,
Winter's magic begins to flow.

Every branch holds a crystal crown,
Nature's beauty in a snowy gown.
Softer than winter's chilly breath,
A tranquil peace that conquers death.

With each snowfall, the world renews,
Painting wishes in sparkling hues.
A serene heart in the wintry chill,
In this softness, I find my will.

Stronger than Night

Among the shadows, where secrets hide,
Whispers gather, a rising tide.
Yet in the depth of the darkening gloom,
A spirit thrives, refusing to doom.

The moon stands guard, a sentinel bright,
Casting a glow on the edge of night.
With courage woven in silver threads,
It lights the path where the weary treads.

Stars flicker on in defiant cheer,
Daring the darkness to draw near.
With steadfast hearts and dreams in flight,
We'll stand our ground, stronger than night.

Each heartbeat echoes in time's embrace,
With hope unfolding, a warm embrace.
In shadows deep, we learn to rise,
Embracing strength beneath the skies.

For in our souls, a fire ignites,
Illuminating the longest nights.
Together we shine, come what may,
Stronger than night as we find our way.

A Melody of Ice on a Fading Horizon

As twilight dances on icy seas,
A melody plays in the cold breeze.
Each note drifts softly, crystal clear,
Caressing the night, drawing us near.

Reflections shimmer on a frozen lake,
The world holds breath, poised for a wake.
Nature sings in harmonious tones,
Whispers echo, beneath the stones.

With each passing moment, colors fade,
Like dreams slipping into the shade.
Yet in this twilight, a beauty glows,
In the heart where the melody flows.

Time spins gently on silken threads,
A tapestry of moments spreads.
Chasing shadows as currents rise,
A symphony beneath endless skies.

In the distance, horizons blur,
Where day and dream begin to stir.
This fleeting song will your heart require,
A melody of ice that won't expire.

Tranquil Reflections on a Frozen Lake

In stillness lies the frozen peace,
A liquid glass where ripples cease.
Mirroring skies of azure bright,
The world distilled in pure delight.

Gentle whispers trace the shore,
Echoes of memories, and so much more.
Trees stand guard, silhouettes stark,
Their limbs adorned with winter's mark.

Here, time flows with a tranquil grace,
Cradling dreams in its soft embrace.
The surface glistens, a soft bouquet,
Reflecting beauty in a subtle way.

As dusk descends and shadows blend,
The calm requires no need to pretend.
Nature's peace wraps 'round like a shawl,
Inviting you to pause, to recall.

On this canvas, the heart finds rest,
In tranquil reflections, we are blessed.
A frozen lake, a quiet song,
In this moment, we all belong.

Twilight in Snowy Realms

Soft whispers of night begin to creep,
The snowflakes dance, in silence they leap.
Moonlight glimmers on a frozen stream,
A world transformed, like a waking dream.

Pine trees stand, draped in silver lace,
Their shadows stretch, a serene embrace.
Stars twinkle high in the deep, dark sky,
In twilight's glow, we feel time fly.

Footprints mark where wanderers tread,
Nature's canvas, painted in red.
The chilly air wraps us like a hug,
In this snowy realm, we feel so snug.

Frost-kissed branches swaying with grace,
Each flake a wonder, no two trace.
Whispers of twilight fill the cold air,
In the snowy realm, we've lost all care.

Serenity reigns in this quiet land,
We wander together, hand in hand.
The night's calm embrace, a soothing balm,
In twilight's hold, the world feels calm.

Harmony in the Chill

A gentle breath of winter's grace,
Quietly descends, a soft embrace.
The world is hushed, in peaceful sleep,
While icy breezes in silence sweep.

Branches arch, with crystal crowns,
The chilly air, it soothes and drowns.
Under a sky of cobalt blue,
Harmony calls in the frosty view.

Laughter rings in the crisp, cool air,
Children play without a care.
Snowman smiles, and sleds go whizzing,
In this wonderland, joy is glistening.

Clouds drift slowly, like dreams in flight,
Painted in hues of soft twilight.
The earth beneath, a patchwork rhyme,
In this harmony, we're lost in time.

As night descends, the stars awake,
Their twinkling dance, the silence breaks.
In the chill, our hearts align,
In winter's song, together we shine.

Veil of the Ice Queen

Through the woods, a shimmer glows,
A veiled mystery, the cold wind blows.
The Ice Queen stirs in her frozen keep,
As secrets guarded, the shadows weep.

Her palace built of crystal bright,
Draped in frost, a breathtaking sight.
Whispers of power fill the icy air,
A beauty fierce, beyond compare.

The moonlight kisses her porcelain skin,
Echoes of stories where dreams begin.
Each flicker of magic sparkles anew,
In the realm where the ice heart drew.

Amidst the snowflakes, her laughter rings,
An enchanting dance, the winter sings.
With every step, the world turns slow,
The veil of the Ice Queen begins to flow.

Yet deep inside, a longing sighs,
A wish for warmth beneath cold skies.
In every flake, a tale unfolds,
Of love that flourished in the bitter cold.

A Feathered Touch

In the crisp air, a swan glides near,
Its wings whisper secrets, soft and clear.
A tranquil lake reflects the sky,
Where dreams take flight and worries die.

With every stroke, it graces the tide,
A feathered dancer, graceful and wide.
Ripples shimmer where it has flown,
In its presence, we feel less alone.

Underneath a canopy of trees,
The nature's heart beats with the breeze.
With each ripple, the world feels new,
A feathered touch in a gentle hue.

The sun dips low, in a golden glow,
As twilight wraps its velvet flow.
Feathers drift down, like whispers of night,
In this moment, everything feels right.

Nature's symphony sings a sweet tune,
A feathered embrace beneath the moon.
In the quietude, we find our way,
With every feather, we learn to stay.

Enchanted Moments in Winter's Glow

Snowflakes dance like fleeting dreams,
Frosty kisses on the seams.
Whispers of wonder fill the night,
As stars twinkle with pure delight.

Silent paths in shimmering white,
Softly wrapped in silver light.
Moonbeams glisten on frozen streams,
In this wonder, the heart redeems.

The trees adorned in icy lace,
Nature's beauty, a sacred space.
Each breath a cloud in the still air,
In winter's glow, we lose our cares.

Footprints trace where spirits roam,
In fields of white, we feel at home.
The chill ignites a spark of cheer,
Embracing magic, drawing near.

And in the quiet, joy we find,
A moment's peace to soothe the mind.
Each second savored, time stands still,
In winter's arms, we bend to will.

The Solo of an Icy Symphony

Strings of silence weave the air,
Echoes whisper, soft and rare.
An icy breath, a chilling breeze,
Nature plays with graceful ease.

Notes of frost and crystal clear,
Resonating far and near.
The symphony in winter's grasp,
In every flake, a melody clasp.

With each gust, the chorus swells,
A harmony in icy dwells.
Pine trees sway in rhythmic flow,
Their secrets in the breezes blow.

Footsteps crunch in perfect time,
A symphony, a frozen rhyme.
Each note a memory, sharp and bright,
Reflecting winter's fleeting light.

So let us dance upon this stage,
In nature's arms, we turn the page.
The solo sings of winter's thrill,
In icy symphony, we're still.

Reflective Dreams on Frost-Kissed Paths

Amidst the white, the world feels new,
Frost-kissed dreams in every view.
Each step a secret left behind,
In whispers shared, our hearts aligned.

Mirrored branches glisten bright,
In nature's hold, we find our light.
Footprints follow where we've been,
This journey holds the tales within.

Reflections dance in winter's gleam,
Beneath the frost, we chase a dream.
A landscape carved by time's embrace,
In every turn, a trace of grace.

The past and present, intertwined,
In snowy paths, our thoughts unwind.
Each moment savored, held so dear,
In winter's touch, the soul draws near.

So let us walk through icy air,
With open hearts, our stories share.
Reflective dreams on frosty ground,
In every step, new hope is found.

Nightfall's Whisper in a Winter's Glow

As twilight falls, the world holds breath,
In winter's arms, we dance with death.
Whispers swathe the night in peace,
A calm embrace, our worries cease.

The moonrise glows, a lantern bright,
In silver drapery, soft the light.
Shadows stretch on powdered snow,
In this moment, our spirits grow.

Crisp air carries a solemn song,
In every note, we feel we belong.
Stars ignite the velvet sky,
As night enfolds, we dream and sigh.

With every breath, the chill we trace,
A gentle comfort, a warm embrace.
The whisper speaks of peace ahead,
In winter's glow, our fears are shed.

So as night falls, let us be still,
In softest light, we find our will.
This tranquil world, a sacred show,
In nightfall's whisper, we truly glow.

Frosted Melodies in Stillness

In the hush of purest white,
Whispers dance in soft moonlight.
Snowflakes twirl with frosty grace,
Nature's song in icy space.

Trees stand tall with glistening crowns,
Blankets cover sleepy towns.
Winds carry tales from afar,
Each note shines like a bright star.

A tranquil world holds its breath,
Beauty crowns the silent depth.
Melodies in stillness rise,
Echo softly, winter sighs.

The air is crisp, the night is clear,
Hearts beat slow, devoid of fear.
In this peace, we find our way,
Listening to what snowflakes say.

Memories wrapped in chilly air,
Each moment tender, calm, and rare.
Frosted melodies take flight,
In the stillness of the night.

Crystal Harmonies on Silent Nights

Beneath the moon's enchanting glow,
Crystals glisten in a row.
Stars align in harmony,
Whispers weave through every tree.

A blanket of white hugs the ground,
Silent magic all around.
Gentle snowflakes kiss the earth,
Each one holds a winter's mirth.

The night is rich with quiet sounds,
Nature's chorus fills the grounds.
Listen close, let your heart roam,
In this stillness, you are home.

Icicles hang like frozen dreams,
Caught in the glow of silver streams.
Magic dances in the air,
Crystal harmonies everywhere.

As soft shadows drift and sway,
Peaceful dreams find their way.
In these moments, clear and bright,
Silent nights bring pure delight.

Winter's Touch in a Moonlit Dream

Moonlit paths of sparkling light,
Winter's touch brings soft delight.
Every flake, a work of art,
Nature's breath, a tender heart.

Frozen lakes reflect the skies,
Silent stars with watchful eyes.
Dreams arise in frosty breath,
In this stillness, fear is death.

Nighttime whispers secrets old,
In the twilight, stories told.
Glimmers dance on branches bare,
Magic lingers in the air.

A tranquil peace wraps tightly round,
In the silence, hope is found.
Every moment feels like gold,
Winter's dreams, a sight to behold.

Within this spell, we gently sway,
Carried far from the light of day.
A moonlit dream, a silent scheme,
Winter's touch, our softest theme.

Gentle Flurries and Peaceful Rhymes

Gentle flurries grace the skies,
Whirling softly, sweet surprise.
Each flake falls like a soft kiss,
Wrapped in winter's tender bliss.

Whispers of the chilly breeze,
Dance through branches, rustling leaves.
Nature hums a soothing tune,
Underneath the watchful moon.

Snowy blankets cloak the ground,
In their depth, sweet peace is found.
Footsteps crunch, a rhythm mild,
In this world, we are but child.

Candles flicker in the night,
Casting warmth, a tender light.
Stories told by fire's glow,
Flurries swirl, a quiet show.

In this moment, time stands still,
As we bask in winter's thrill.
Gentle flurries, peace entwined,
In this rhymed dance, hearts aligned.

Milton Keynes UK
Ingram Content Group UK Ltd.
UKHW021046031224
452078UK00010B/607

9 789916 797846